THE OFFICIAL
SCOTLAND
FOOTBALL
ANNUAL 2011

SCOTLAND

Written by David Forsyth
Design by David Flockhart

A Grange Publication

© 2010. Published by Grange Communications Ltd., Edinburgh, under licence from The Scottish Football Association.
Printed in the EU.

Photographs © The Scottish FA, The Scottish Football Museum, SNSPix, PA Photos

£7.99

ISBN: 978-1-907104-73-2

CONTENTS

Welcome to The Official Scotland Football Annual 2011 – packed with pictures and information about your national team. The stars of today, the stars of yesterday and the stars of tomorrow all feature, alongside a profile of National Coach Craig Levein, and a look ahead to the remaining fixtures on the road to the European Championships. In addition, you can enjoy a look at how our Women's team is faring, and test your knowledge of Scotland.

To play for your country is the greatest honour that football can bestow, and to pull on the dark blue Scotland jersey has meant an enormous amount to great players down through the decades.

The modern day is no exception, with both our players and National Coach committed to working as hard as they can and making maximum use of their talents to take us to the Finals of the European Championships.

Scotland is looking ahead to a future we all hope will be filled with excitement and opportunity, but it is also useful to look backwards to reflect on our history and where we have come from. This annual does so in two very enjoyable ways: in looking at the history of football's oldest international rivalry, Scotland v England, and by looking at some of the greatest goal scorers to have graced that fixture.

Our game continues to expand its own boundaries, and the development of our international Women's team is also well worth reading about, as is taking the chance to looking at our under 21 and youth talents.

I hope you will enjoy it.

George Peat

THE MANAGER

When the snow-delayed announcement of Craig Levein's appointment as National Coach was made, he quickly made his feelings known.

"As a proud Scotland fan, it is a dream come true to take charge of the national team" he told the media.

The new man at the helm wasted little time in stressing that he hoped to see the pride he felt emulated by others involved in our national game. "I think we need to change attitudes more than anything else, and be a bit more positive about what we are doing.

"We need to instil a bit more pride and passion, and even protect our country when people talk about us, standing up for Scotland when things have not gone so well."

A man known for his strong views and meticulous planning, Craig lost little time in seeking to unite the country behind the team.

Craig Levein's first match in charge saw Scotland take on the talented Czech Republic in a friendly at Hampden, a match which ended in an encouraging 1-0 win for the Scots.

The draw for the UEFA European 2012 Qualifying Round saw Scotland face the most difficult of opponents – with World and reigning European Champions Spain in the same group alongside the Czech Republic, Lithuania and Liechtenstein.

The second round of those matches looms in 2011, with qualification still very much the aim.

He said: "It's a tough group, but an exciting one. All of the fixtures are important, but clearly the matches against Spain capture the imagination."

Craig's coaching career began after he was forced by injury into early retirement as a player. He worked on the coaching staff at Heart of Midlothian and Livingston, before taking his first managerial job at Cowdenbeath in 1997.

In December 2000, he left to take over as Manager at Hearts, the club he graced as a player, and guided them to a third place finish in successive seasons.

His impressive record at Tynecastle led to an approach from Leicester City in October 2004, and he was at the helm of the Championship side until January 2006. He returned to football a few months later, when he took charge of his boyhood heroes, Raith Rovers, and then a few months later was appointed to the hot seat at Dundee United where he spent three successful years before taking up the Scotland position.

Craig Levein Factfile:

Name: **Craig William Levein**
Born: **October 22nd, 1964**
Place: **Dunfermline, Scotland**
School: **Inverkeithing High (where he played alongside another future Scotland star, Gordon Durie)**

Height: **6ft 1in**
Position: **Defender**
Clubs as a player: **Cowdenbeath (1981-83) appearances 60; Hearts (1983-1995) appearances 329**

Clubs Managed: **Cowdenbeath (1997-2000); Hearts (2000-2004); Leicester City (2004-2006); Raith Rovers (2006); Dundee United (2006 – 2009)**

Levein the Player:

Craig signed for Cowdenbeath from Junior club Lochore Welfare in 1981, and quickly established himself in the first-team at Central Park.

A cultured central defender, he quickly caught the eye of bigger teams and in 1983 he moved to Hearts for a reported fee of £40,000.

Again, his ability quickly ensured a regular first-team slot and in 1985 and 1986, he was named the SPFA Young Player of the Year.

He made his Scotland debut in a 1-0 win against Argentina at Hampden in March

1990, playing well enough to secure a place in the 1990 World Cup squad. He went on to win 16 caps, and would have added to that tally but for two serious knee injuries which eventually forced him into early retirement.

Later this year the second round of qualifying fixtures for the European Championships 2012 kicks off.

We take a look at the matches that will decide Scotland's fate, and at the star names set to face Scotland.

Czech Republic
Hampden Park, September 3rd

As ever, the Czechs will present a formidable hurdle. A team packed with technically gifted players, many of whom play at the highest levels of European club football.

Fixtures between Scotland and the Czech Republic are historically tight affairs, with little to separate the two nations in the head to head.

Two of the stars who will be hoping to put Scotland to the sword are well known to followers of the English Premiership.

Tomas Rosicky, the cultured and talented attacking midfielder, plays his trade for Arsenal. His club manager has described him as a player with "remarkable vision." He has earned his nickname of "The Little Mozart" for his ability to orchestrate matches from midfield.

With more than 70 caps and around 20 goals to his name since making his debut in 2000 at the age of 19, he presents a real threat to Scottish progress.

Petr Cech stands a forbidding 6ft 5ins tall and has been a dominant figure in Chelsea's goal since making the breakthrough into the first team in 2004 when Carlo Cudicini was injured.

He was named in the All-Star team at Euro 2004 after helping his team reach the semi-finals. The big keeper holds a number of Premiership and Czech international records for clean sheets and also has more than 70 caps.

Lithuania
Hampden Park, September 6th

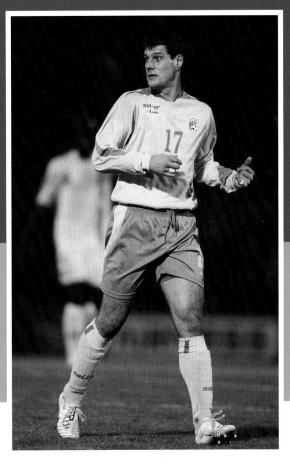

Two of Lithuania's star players are very well known to football fans in Scotland, and will be hoping to turn the tables on the nation where they have plied their trade.

While Scotland has the better record in fixtures between the two nations, the matches have all been hard fought encounters.

Marius Zaliukas is the big central defender who has been a rock in the Hearts defence since signing for the Tynecastle Club in 2006.

At 6ft 3 ins tall, he is an imposing player but one who is comfortable enough on the ball to perform in midfield when asked to do so. He has played more than 20 times for his country.

Injury has hit the Rangers career of striker **Andrius Velicka** since he signed on at Ibrox from Viking Stavanger in 2008. Even so, in just eight appearances he has managed to hit the net four times.

His scoring record in Scotland has been excellent. In a spell at Hearts from 2006-2008, the burly striker scored 19 goals in 47 appearances. He has more than 20 caps.

Liechtenstein away, October 8th

Liechtenstein played its first unofficial international match in 1981, a 1-1 draw against Malta. The first official international played by Liechtenstein came two years later in a 0-1 defeat to Switzerland.

While the minnows of the group, history shows no team deserves to be underestimated and Liechtenstein has earned World Cup qualifying draws against talented Portugal.

They will be looking to a strong Swiss connection to see them through the campaign.

Undoubted star of the side is **Mario Frick** (pictured above), a striker who plays in the Swiss Super League for FC St Gallen.

His cap haul is approaching 100, and his career has taken him to a number of top Swiss sides, including Basel and FC Zurich and also to Serie A side Verona.

Martin Buchel is signed with FC Zurich, and has around 30 caps. The talented midfielder is viewed as one of his nation's brightest young footballing talents and made his international debut at the tender age of 17.

Spain
away, October 11th

What a prospect for the Tartan Army to savour - an away trip to the home of the greatest footballing power on earth at the moment, the reigning European and World Champions.

A galaxy of stars has seen the Spanish dominate international football with their beautiful passing game, but perhaps two deserve special mention, with both playing for Barcelona.

Attacking midfielder **Andres Iniesta** struck the winning goal in the World Cup Final. Known in the Spanish media as "Don Andres" or "El Cerebro" (the Brain) the little midfielder has earned a half

century of caps as an integral part of the most talented midfield on earth.

Many pundits, including Manchester United's Wayne Rooney, believe Iniesta to be the best player in the world.

David Villa is another World Cup winner, and his haul of goals helped Spain reach the Final. Rapidly approaching 70 caps, he is destined to be his nation's greatest ever international goal scorer.

He is, statistically, the world's top goal scorer at international level.

It's the oldest international rivalry in football – a match that generates more passion and interest than almost any other.

Once an annual event, it is a fixture that now has to take its place in the jam-packed international arena. Scotland v England is still a prospect that whets the appetite of football fans on both sides of the border, and with good reason.

Some rare classics have been served up since the fixture was first played, and honours are pretty evenly matched. In the 110 fixtures, England has emerged victorious on 45 occasions, Scotland on 41 and there have been 24 draws. We look back at some highlights…

International Football Begins…

Wembley Wizards

When Scotland met England on November 30th in 1872 it was not just the first time the two sides had met, it was also the first official International football match. The match fell on St Andrew's Day and was played at the West of Scotland cricket club's ground in Glasgow.

Uniquely, all of Scotland's players were from Queen's Park F.C. England's players were selected from nine different clubs. A crowd of 4000 watched the game, which finished 0-0.

The Wembley Wizards

In 1928, Scotland gave perhaps their greatest performance against England at Wembley.

Alex Jackson headed the opener after just three minutes and, despite a strong defensive performance from England, Alex James added the second just before half time with a left foot shot.

Remarkably, Scotland played even better after the break, dominating play with a thrilling attacking display. Jackson added a third with a header. Alex James then scored his second and as the game neared its end Alex Jackson completed his hat-trick before England scored a late consolation.

With a final score of England 1, Scotland 5, the legendary performance of Scotland saw them dubbed the "Wembley Wizards".

Alex Jackson

World Record Crowd

In 1937, Scotland and England set a new world record at the time for attendance at a football match. The official Hampden crowd was given as 149,415, though the unofficial attendance is thought to be even higher. The figure remains a European record to this day.

The day was complete with the beating of England 3-1. Bob McPhail scored twice and Francis O'Donnell once for the Scots.

Bob McPhail

THE WORLD'S OLDEST RIVALRY –

Scotland as World Champions

While there is an argument that the 1928 Wembley win was Scotland's greatest victory against England, the famous Wembley clash of 1967 is undoubtedly Scotland's most famous victory over the Auld Enemy.

England had been crowned World Champions in 1966 and went into this game on the back of a 19 match unbeaten run. They were hot favourites, but Scotland had a strong side featuring four of Celtic's legendary "Lisbon Lions" as well as greats Jim Baxter, Denis Law and Billy Bremner.

"The Lawman" opened the scoring for Scotland, netting from close range. Bobby Lennox doubled the advantage on 78 minutes before Jack Charlton scored for England. Scotland debutant Jim McCalliog netted to make it 3-1 to the Scots before Geoff Hurst hit back to make it 3-2.

But it was the nature of the win, rather than the scoreline, that delighted all of Scotland. As the match drew to a close, Rangers legend Jim Baxter began playing "keepie uppie" at walking pace, tormenting England and their support.

Billy Bremner and Jim Baxter

Billy Bremner

Denis Law

1976 and THAT goal

More than 85,000 were packed in to Hampden to see Scotland take on England in the home internationals. The match was finely poised at 1-1, when England goalkeeping legend Ray Clemence was famously nutmegged by Scotland's record caps holder, Kenny Dalglish, for a famous 2-1 win.

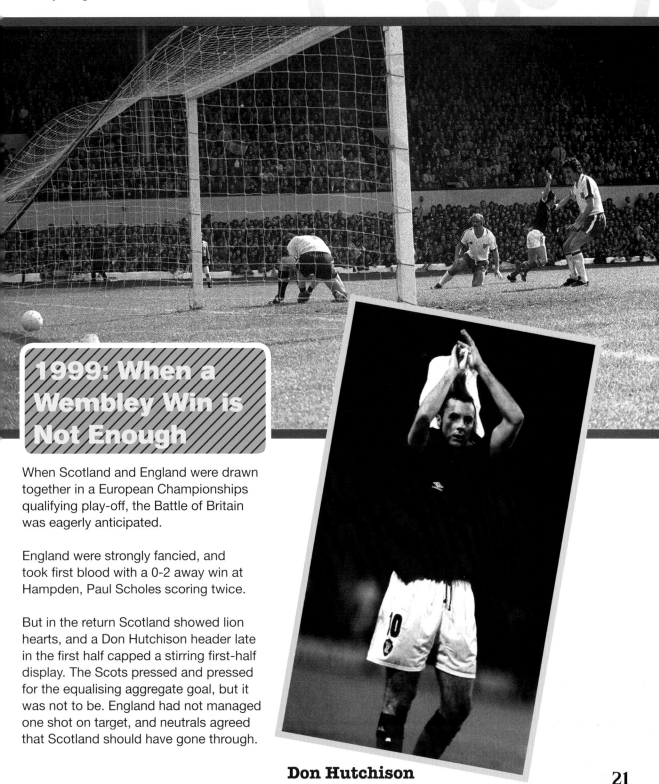

1999: When a Wembley Win is Not Enough

When Scotland and England were drawn together in a European Championships qualifying play-off, the Battle of Britain was eagerly anticipated.

England were strongly fancied, and took first blood with a 0-2 away win at Hampden, Paul Scholes scoring twice.

But in the return Scotland showed lion hearts, and a Don Hutchison header late in the first half capped a stirring first-half display. The Scots pressed and pressed for the equalising aggregate goal, but it was not to be. England had not managed one shot on target, and neutrals agreed that Scotland should have gone through.

Don Hutchison

21

1. Who is Scotland's most-capped player?

2. Who is Scotland's most-capped goalkeeper?

3. Which club side is Billy Bremner most associated with?

4. Which county does Craig Levein come from?

5. Against which country did Archie Gemmill score his "greatest ever" goal for Scotland?

6. Which Scotland star scored a stunning goal to defeat France in Paris in 2007?

7. Which German World Cup winner has managed Scotland?

8. At which club did goalkeeper Craig Gordon play when he was first capped?

Answers on p 61.

Craig Levein

Billy Bremner

KENNY DALGLISH

Ask any Scotland fan to name the nation's greatest-ever international goal scorer and there's a fair chance the first name to escape their lips will be "Kenny Dalglish."

But while Scotland's most-capped player sits proudly atop the goal-scoring list with 30 goals for his country (equal with Denis Law), he was not the most prolific of all time, notching his 30 in his magnificent 102 cap career.

Neither was "The Lawman", taking 55 appearances to reach his total – although his goals-to-games ratio does see him force his way into our top three.

We take a look at this hat-trick of goal-scoring legends, whose ability to find the net makes them our scoring idols.

HUGHIE GALLACHER

Hughie Gallacher scored an astonishing 23 goals in just 20 international appearances – an astonishing 115% goals-to-games ratio.

This makes him the most prolific striker ever to wear a Scotland jersey.

Hughie played in the 1920s and 30s, his career spanning 624 senior games for a whole host of clubs in Scotland and England. He was, famously, one of the Wembley Wizards who beat England 5-1 in 1928.

Although standing just 5ft 5ins tall, Hugh could strike the ball powerfully with either foot, dribble and head. Born in Lanarkshire, his boyhood friends included another who was to become a "Wizard", Alex James.

He played with Queen of the South and Airdrieonians in Scotland before earning his move to Newcastle United, where he enjoyed the finest spell of his career scoring 133 goals in 160 league appearances. He also enjoyed spells at Chelsea, Derby County and Notts County.

In his career, Hughie scored an incredible 463 goals in his 624 matches. He died in tragic circumstances in 1957.

Lawrie Reilly was a key component of Hibernian's feared "Famous Five" forward line – Smith, Johnstone, Reilly, Turnbull and Ormond – which lit up Scottish, British and European football in the 1950s.

A one-club man, he grew up to play for the team he and his family supported, and remains Hibernian's most capped player.

In his 38 appearances for Scotland, Lawrie scored 22 goals – pushing him into second place in our "most prolific" chart with a goals-to-games ratio of 58%.

He won the first of his caps against Wales, but it was against England that Lawrie was to make his reputation and earn his soubriquet "Last Minute Reilly." In all, he scored five goals in four consecutive appearances for Scotland against England at Wembley. His second goal in the final seconds of the 2-2 draw in 1953 earned him his nickname.

Lawrie made 253 league appearances for Hibernian, scoring 185 goals along with a further 47 in cup ties and other appearances.

He remains a very regular attender at his beloved Easter Road.

Denis Law, "The Lawman", remains a Scottish goal-scoring legend as well as a hero to football fans in Manchester.

Born in Aberdeen in 1940, his career encompassed three decades – the 50s, 60s and 70s – and saw him play in Scotland, England and Italy.

He is best known for the time he spent at Manchester United, from 1962 – 1973 and remains the only Scottish player to have won the prestigious European Footballer of the Year Award (1964).

Denis won 55 caps, scoring 30 goals to place him first equal on the goals scored charts, and he sits in third-place in our "most prolific" list with a goals-to-games ratio of 54.5%.

A player who smashed transfer fee records on three occasions, Denis is also Manchester United's second highest scorer behind Sir Bobby Charlton, and once netted 46 times in one season.

He played for Scotland from 1958 till 1974, when he represented his country in the World Cup.

LAWRIE REILLY

Wembley, 1967, England 2 - 3 Scotland

DENIS LAW

The development of talented young footballers capable of competing on the international stage remains a strong priority.

And Scotland has achieved considerable success in competing at the various youth levels, most notably reaching the Final of the European under 19 Championships in 2006 only to lose to a strong Spanish side 2-1.

Qualification for the later stages of tournaments has regularly been achieved at youth levels, and that in itself is an achievement. However the aim of blooding young players from the under 15 age group onwards has a wider remit.

Ross Mathie, International Youth Team Coach, explains: "The aim is to provide young players with an opportunity to test themselves at international level from a fairly young age.

"In turn, that allows them to compete against the best players from around Europe and the World, to learn and develop as professional footballers and as young men. They learn how to cope with travelling, with meeting new people, and with not being an automatic first pick and learning to be part of a squad.

"Most of all, what we are dealing with is potential, and trying to help young players realise that potential."

There is a strong history of players progressing through the ranks at youth level. For every late international bloomer, like James McFadden, Ross can point to a series of others, such as Gary Caldwell and Darren Fletcher, who have worked up through the various youth level ranks. Protecting young players from undue pressures, and keeping feet firmly planted on the floor, is also a task for coaches at both club and international level. For that

ROSS MATHIE

reason, Ross is loath to start publicly identifying young players with outstanding ability at too early a stage.

However, he was prepared to identify one or two talents to watch in the years ahead.

Jack Grimmer became the youngest ever Aberdeen player to play in the full team when he made his debut in April 2010 against Rangers at Ibrox. It may have surprised one or two Dons fans, but it didn't surprise Ross.

He said: "He had captained our under 16 side from midfield, and he has fantastic potential. He followed hard in the footsteps of his team-mate Fraser Fyvie, who had captained the Scotland under 16s before Jack and had also made his first-team breakthrough at Aberdeen very young. Fraser is now an established first-teamer, and Jack could well do the same."

At under 19 levels, Scotland have a number of players already turning out regularly for their clubs – including Fraser Fyvie, John Fleck of Rangers, and Paul Slane at Celtic.

Hearts striker Scott Robinson is one of the youngest players ever to play in the SPL, and in his hatful of appearances has already scored. He has played for Scotland from under 16s onwards.

His club team-mate Craig Thomson is now a regular full-back starter who is pushing on at international level.

The youth system operates from under 15s up to under 18s under the tutelage of Ross, with the under 19s and under 21s being the responsibility of Billy Stark. Ross confirms there is considerable crossover in conversation, however. He said: "Once players are getting into the under 21 level, then clearly we are working with players who are often regularly appearing for their club and who we are hoping can make the big step to become full international players.

"In recent years we have seen a lot of players make that step – guys like Steven Fletcher, Scott Brown and Stevie Naismith.

"I hope that shows that we are still producing good footballers, it's not all doom and gloom!"

1. Who was the last Manager to lead Scotland to the Finals of a major championship?

2. Name the Manchester United star who captained Scotland last season?

3. Which nation topped Scotland's qualifying group for World Cup 2010?

4. Against which nation did Scotland record our biggest ever international win, and what was the score?

5. Name the Scottish defender who has won most caps?

6. How many times has Scotland competed at the World Cup Finals?

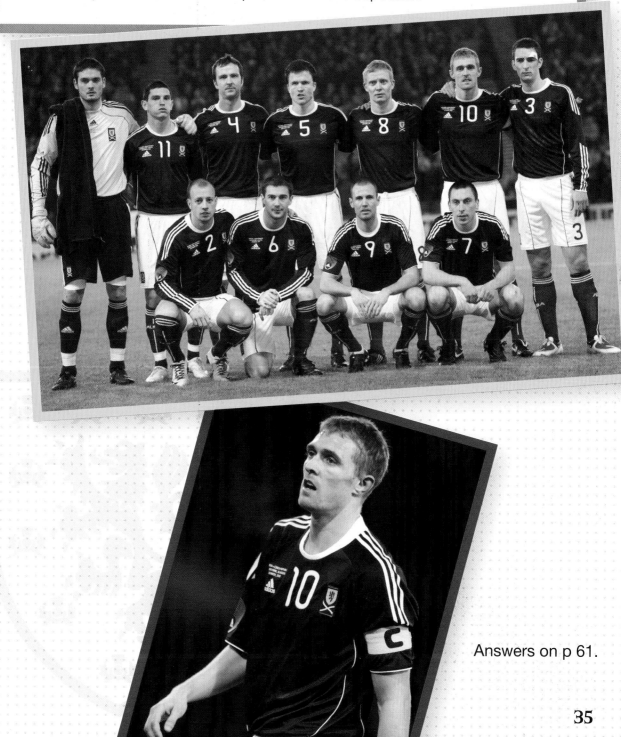

Answers on p 61.

CRAIG GORDON

Craig Gordon is one of the best goalkeepers in the British game, playing in the top flight in England against some of the world's best strikers.

The big keeper, who stands 6ft 4ins tall, is a lifelong Hearts fan, where he began his career and developed his reputation before his move south to Sunderland for a fee reported to be £9million – a British record for a goalkeeper.

He made his top class debut for Hearts in 2002, and has since won a string of honours and awards.

Agile, commanding and brave, his performances for Scotland earned him rave notices and brought him to the attention of managers down south, where he is now highly regarded by leading figures in the game.

Gary Caldwell is a cornerstone of Scotland's defence, and although mainly used as a central defender his ability on the ball has also seen him deployed as a holding midfielder.

A reliable performer, Caldwell is also one of the leaders in the team, constantly urging on his team-mates and organising those around him.

Matches against France are engraved in his own personal international history. Gary made his debut against France in Paris in a 5-1 defeat under Berti Vogts, but more memorably scored the only goal of the game in the 1-0 victory against the French in the Euro 2008 qualifying match at Hampden in 2006.

Gary Caldwell began his career at Newcastle United, but made his big breakthrough after a move to Hibernian. He then played in championship winning sides at Celtic, before moving to Wigan.

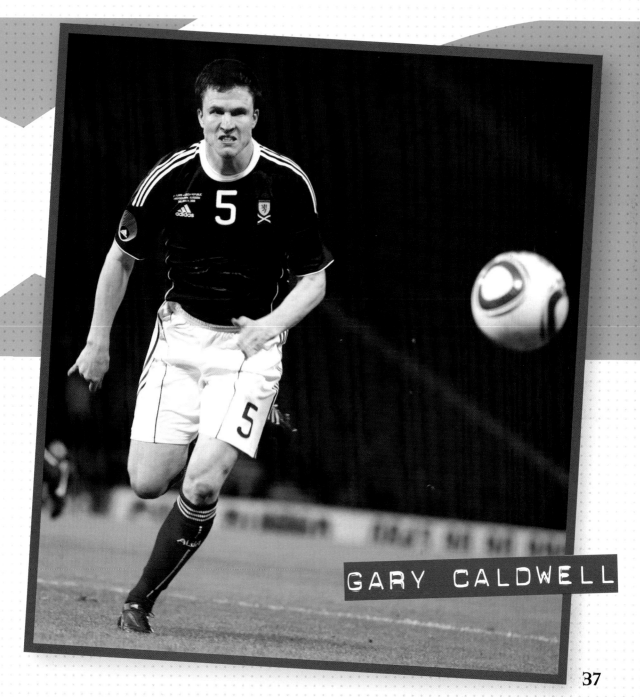

GARY CALDWELL

ALAN HUTTON

Alan Hutton is a thoroughly modern full-back, strong in defence and providing a wide attacking outlet.

His move south to Spurs from Rangers, where his career had been carefully developed, followed a number of outstanding performances at international level which drew praise from several top managers, including Sir Alex Ferguson.

Alan has come through the levels, playing for Scotland's under 21 and B sides before making his top team breakthrough under Alex McLeish in May 2007 in a friendly against Austria. His competitive debut came shortly afterwards against Lithuania.

International highlights include his part in the memorable win against France at the Parc des Princes in September 2007.

Christophe Berra is another Scot now playing in England's top flight, the central defender part of the rearguard at Wolves.

A rugged 6ft 3ins tall, the former Hearts man has been capped at a variety of age levels.

He made his international debut as a substitute in a friendly match in Prague against the Czech Republic in May 2008. His first start came almost a year later, when he turned out for Scotland against the Netherlands in Amsterdam in March 2009.

Christophe, whose middle name is Didier, was also eligible to play for France through his father's side of the family.

CHRISTOPHE BERRA

Graham Dorrans proved to be something of a surprise package when Tony Mowbray took him south to West Bromwich Albion in 2008.

The young midfielder's move from Livingston virtually passed unnoticed – but not for long. A series of man of the match performances in the past two seasons has seen Graham become one of the players of the English Championship, and he played a key role in the successful push for promotion to the Premier League.

Graham has also played for his country at a variety of levels, and was called into the squad for the match against the Netherlands in September 2009 before making his debut a month later in a friendly against Japan.

He made his home debut in the 1-0 win over the Czech Republic in March 2010, earning the man of the match award for his efforts.

GRAHAM DORRANS

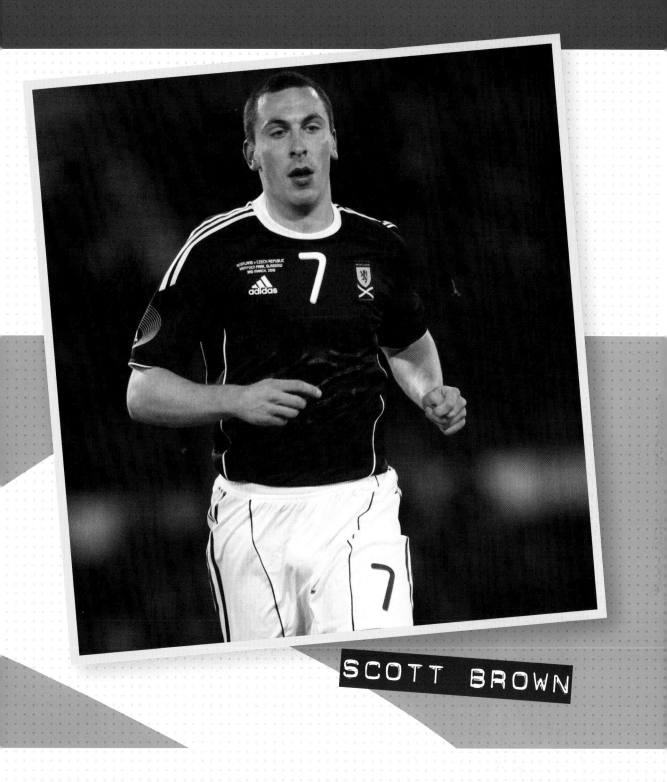

SCOTT BROWN

Scott Brown is an all-action, bustling midfield player who is now a key part of the engine room alongside skipper Darren Fletcher.

Now an established internationalist with more than 20 caps, Scott made his debut when he came on as a sub against the USA in November 2005.

He has scored two international goals, his first against Macedonia in September 2009 in a World Cup qualifying match at Hampden, and the second coming in a friendly against the Czech Republic.

Scott began his career at Hibernian, coming through that club's lauded youth system with fellow internationalists Kevin Thomson, Steven Whittaker, Gary O'Connor, Steven Fletcher and Derek Riordan, before moving to Celtic for a record transfer between two Scottish clubs.

Another of the Scots now gracing England's top flight, Charlie Adam was an integral part of the Blackpool side that took the Championship by surprise, gaining promotion to the Premier League through the play-offs. A gifted left foot and an intelligent football brain have seen the former Ranger force his way back into the international reckoning, creating even more competition in the midfield area.

Since his move south, he has enjoyed a new lease of life, gaining a regular place in the now Premier League side and testing his skills in that competitive environment week in and week out.

In addition to his general play, Charlie's ability from dead balls makes him a potent threat.

CHARLIE ADAM

James McFadden is a player who can produce a moment of brilliance to turn a match.

He can operate as a striker, playing through the centre, an attacking midfielder or as a wide player.

Never was that ability to produce more evident than in September 2007, when a stunning long-range strike in Paris saw Scotland win 1-0 on French soil during the World Cup qualifying campaign.

That wonder goal, and other important strikes, has seen the former Motherwell star who now plays for Birmingham City in the English Premier League become a firm favourite of the Tartan Army.

JAMES MCFADDEN

43

Kenny Miller is Mr Perpetual Motion.

The Rangers star works tirelessly for the international team, often leading the line with great energy and commitment and giving defenders no chance to settle.

Now very experienced, Kenny made his debut for Craig Brown's Scotland in 2001 in a match against Poland, and has since remained a constant presence under managers Berti Vogts, Walter Smith, Alex McLeish, George Burley and now Craig Levein.

He has scored goals in crucial games, including strikes against Germany, Ukraine, Austria, Italy and Norway.

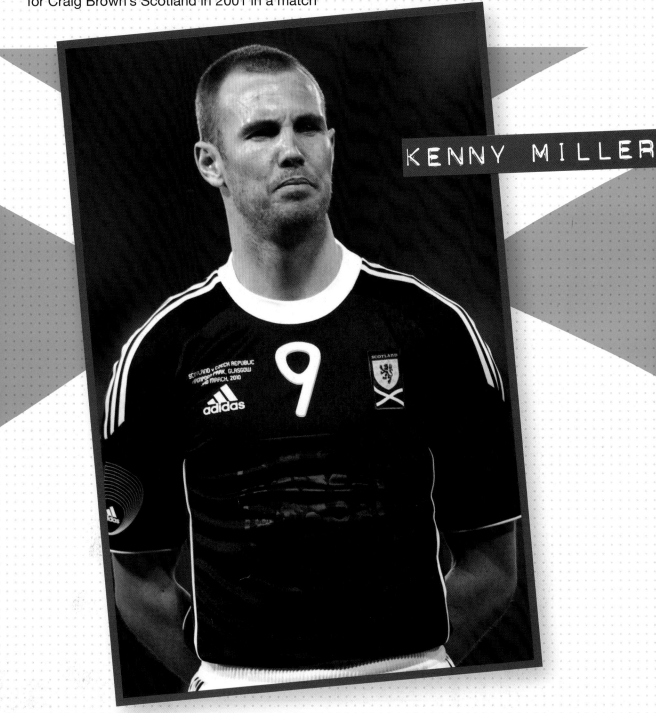

KENNY MILLER

Steven Fletcher has developed into one of the lynchpins of the Scottish attack.

The striker is big, quick, and brave with a skilful and powerful left foot. He now plays in the English Premier League with Wolves, after moving from Burnley last summer for more than £7 million.

Steven has worked his way up through the international ranks, having been capped at various levels including under 20, under 21 and B level. He was the top scorer in the under 19 side which reached the final of the European Championships in 2006, losing to Spain in the final.

He made his breakthrough into the full side against Croatia in March 2008, when he provided the assist for Kenny Miller's goal in a 1-1 draw. He scored his first full international goal in a 2-1 win against Iceland in April 2009.

STEVEN FLETCHER

CAPTAIN FLETCHER

Darren Fletcher seems to make a habit of proving his doubters wrong.

First up were sceptical Manchester United fans, many of whom initially felt the gangling midfielder was not of the quality of some of those who have previously worn the famous red jersey.

Fortunately, that was never a view shared by the one man whose view counts most, his manager Sir Alex Ferguson. And the maestro's faith in Fletcher has paid off handsomely, as a series of stellar performances over the past two or three seasons have seen his stock soar.

The story has been broadly the same in the dark blue of Scotland, with increasingly mature and influential performances gradually winning over any lingering doubters.

What many forget, of course, is that even with around 50 caps to his name, Fletcher is still a relatively young man with many years at the top level ahead of him. Remember, this is a man who first captained his country at just 20 years of age.

When he was made captain of his country, the Dalkeith born Fletcher was justifiably delighted. "It means everything to me to lead the team out."

Darren's preferred position, of course, is in the central midfield role he fills so effectively for both United and Scotland. But he can also play wide right, right back and has even turned out in central defence.

But his versatility shouldn't detract from the quality he brings to his preferred role. United team-mate Wayne Rooney describes the Scotland captain as "a world-class player and I wouldn't swap him for any other in the world."

The player himself is more modest in his view: "I try to get on the ball, trying to control the game and make things happen. Most games are won because of the way you control games in midfield. From there you can dictate the game and dominate possession."

The captain leads by example, his endless dedication to the cause and his ability to drift into dangerous areas seeing him score a number of important goals.

And with his best years perhaps still to come, the Tartan Army can look forward to seeing a lot more of Skipper Fletcher.

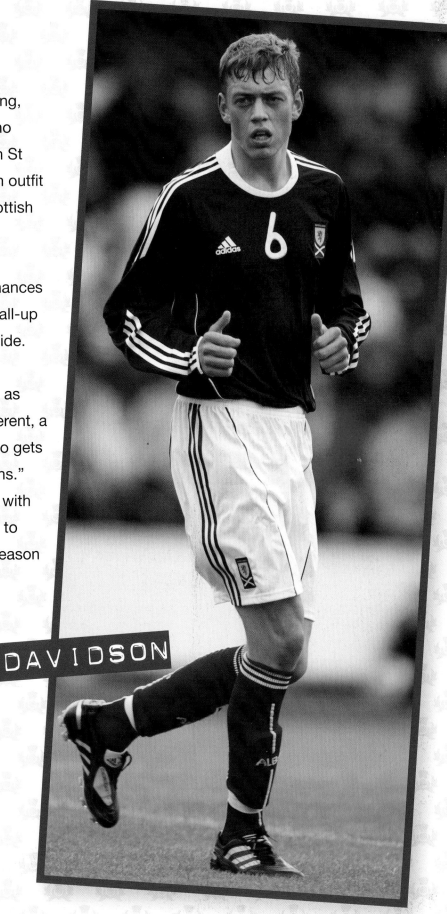

Murray Davidson is a strong, high-energy midfielder who has been a revelation with St Johnstone since the Perth outfit won promotion to the Scottish Premier League.

A string of strong performances has seen Murray earn a call-up to Billy Stark's under 21 side.

The coach described him as "giving us something different, a box-to-box midfielder who gets into good scoring positions." Murray started his career with Livingston before moving to the Saints at the end of season 2008-09.

MURRAY DAVIDSON

Kevin McDonald has made many appearances for the under 21 side, the Burnley midfielder now operating on the fringes of the full national squad.

Big, strong and skilful, he first made his name with Dundee, before earning a big move to Burnley in the English Championship in 2008.

A season in the top flight followed after Burnley won promotion, and McDonald made regular appearances in the side where he performed consistently.

KEVIN MCDONALD

David Goodwillie is one of the most talked about young players in Scotland, following a string of strong performances last season culminating in a goal-scoring feat as his Dundee United won the Scottish Cup.

He has played for his country at all youth levels, and is an important member of the under 21 squad.

The young striker is quick, skilful and aggressive and his high level of performance has attracted much interest.

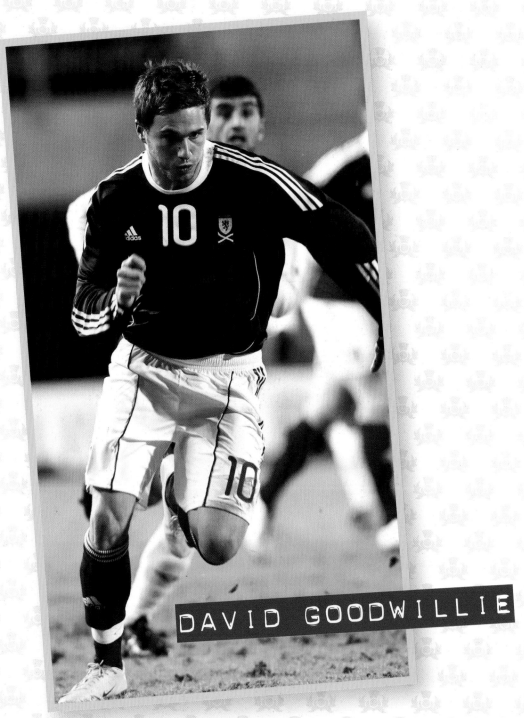

DAVID GOODWILLIE

David Wotherspoon has graduated from the Hibernian youth academy into the Easter Road first-team with apparent ease.

A skilful and versatile player, his achievements for his club saw him earn a place in the under 21 squad after already representing Scotland at under 18 and under 19 levels.

He made his debut last season in a 4-0 win against Azerbaijan.

DAVID
WOTHERSPOON

(top left: Alex McLeish, top right: Jim Leighton and bottom: Danny McGrain)

Kenny Dalglish	102
Jim Leighton	91
Alex McLeish	77
Paul McStay	76
Thomas Boyd	72
Christian Dailly	69
David Weir	65
Willie Miller	65
Danny McGrain	62
Ally McCoist	61
Richard Gough	61
John Collins	58
Gary McAllister	57
Roy Aitken	57
Denis Law	55
Maurice Malpas	55
Billy Bremner	54
Graeme Souness	54
Alan Rough	53
George Young	53
Kevin Gallacher	53
Joe Jordan	52
Colin Hendry	51
Asa Hartford	50
Gordon Strachan	50
Darren Fletcher	50

Anna Signeul has seen great strides in the five years she has been at the helm of the women's game in Scotland.

The hugely experienced Swede is the Scotland Women's National Coach, and has presided over a steady increase in the quality and quantity of women and girls turning to the beautiful game.

That has seen an improvement in the fortunes for the national team, and the emergence of a fresh crop of talented players to follow in the footsteps of the renowned Julie Fleeting.

It is a virtuous cycle that Anna would like to see continue, and indeed quicken in pace. And she knows that in Scotland the national team are very much the standard bearers for the sport.

"We really want to qualify for a major championship final. That will see the sport gain much more attention, and that will help encourage more women to take up football.

"There is such tremendous interest in football in Scotland that any success can only benefit our game.

"In the men's game, there is huge interest in the clubs – especially in the Premier League – as well as in how the national team does. For us, the focus is very much more on the national team.

"In that regard it is important that there are role models playing in the national team, and we are fortunate in that we do have such players in Scotland. For example, Kim Little and Jennifer Beattie have now joined Julie Fleeting in playing for the excellent Arsenal Ladies team.

"We are also seeing the emergence of another raft of talented players – for example Rachel Corsie has done fantastically well since making the step up from the under 19 team and is another to watch."

With more than 100 caps and goals for her country, Julie Fleeting puts captaining her country down amongst her proudest moments. An iconic figure in the game, she continues to inspire other women and girls to take up the sport.

Anna said: "These role models can help to inspire more girls to take up football, but it is also important that clubs are there to help them develop and get the enjoyment they want from the sport.

"It is fantastic that in Scotland we have professional clubs, like Celtic, Rangers and Hibernian all involved increasingly in the women's game, offering fantastic facilities and help. These clubs have an infrastructure in place that the women can buy into.

"But it is also terrific that we have clubs like Glasgow City, the league winners and now playing in the Champions League, which is not attached to any professional club but still conducts itself in a very serious way. The club has a full-time coach, the players train every evening and play on Sundays. The Club wants to improve, and to be really one of the best clubs in Europe."

Kim Little:

A midfielder who now stars for Arsenal, Kim made her name at Hibernian Ladies from 2006-2008.

She has made around 30 appearances for her country.

She has made more than 50 appearances for Arsenal, and in her first full season down south was named the club's Players Player of the Year.

She is an assured midfielder, with a football intellect far beyond her years. Anna Signeul, her national coach, said: "Kim is an exceptional talent. She has great natural ability, but she has been training and working really hard to develop and improve."

Rachel Corsie:

Rachel so impressed coach Anna Signeul after stepping up from the under 19s to play centre half in the full Scotland side, that she has stayed there ever since.

A strong all-round player, good in the air and comfortable on the ball, Rachel is the epitome of a modern defender.

One of several Glasgow City players in the Scotland set-up, Rachel also captained the country at under 19 level.

Anna said: "She has been very impressive since she broke into the team. Rachel really is one to watch."

SCOTTISH FA FACEBOOK PAGE

www.facebook.com/scotlandnationalteam

The Scotland National Team facebook page provides Scotland supporters with a fantastic opportunity to catch up on all the news and chat about their favourite players and the team. A host of features includes exclusive video and chat forum.

Quiz – p 22

1. Who is Scotland's most-capped player?
Kenny Dalglish

2. Who is Scotland's most-capped goalkeeper?
Jim Leighton

3. Which club side is Billy Bremner most associated with? Leeds United

4. Which county does Craig Levein come from? Fife

5. Against which country did Archie Gemmill score his "greatest ever" goal for Scotland? The Netherlands

6. Which Scotland star scored a stunning goal to defeat France in Paris in 2007? James McFadden

7. Which German World Cup winner has managed Scotland? Berti Vogts

8. At which club did goalkeeper Craig Gordon play when he was first capped? Hearts

Quiz – p 35

1. Who was the last Manager to lead Scotland to the finals of a major championship? Craig Brown

2. Name the Manchester United star who captained Scotland last season? Darren Fletcher

3. Which nation topped Scotland's qualifying group for World Cup 2010? The Netherlands

4. Against which nation did Scotland record our biggest ever international win, and what was the score? Ireland, 11-0 in 1901

5. Name the Scottish defender who has won most caps? Alex McLeish

6. How many times has Scotland competed at the World Cup Finals? 8

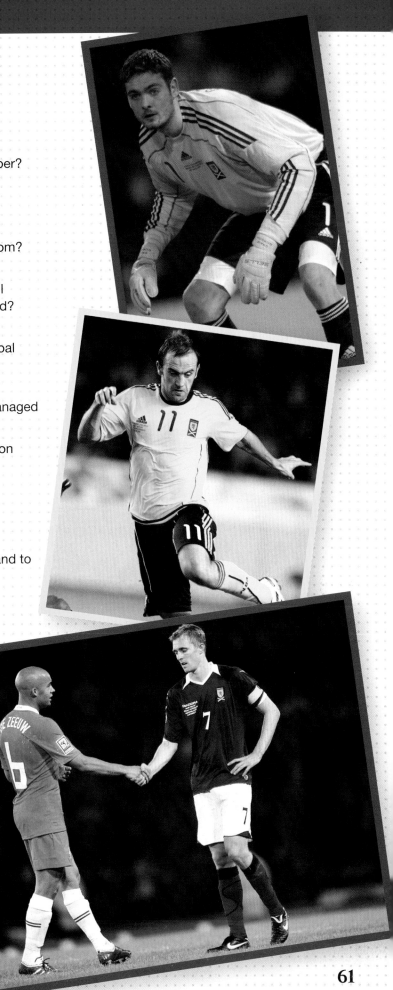

61